PILOT

People I Meet

DOUGLAS BENDER

A Crabtree Roots Book

Crabtree Publishing
crabtreebooks.com

School-to-Home Support for Caregivers and Teachers

This book helps children grow by letting them practice reading. Here are a few guiding questions to help the reader with building his or her comprehension skills. Possible answers appear here in red.

Before Reading:

- What do I think this book is about?
    - *I think this book is about pilots.*
    - *I think this book will tell me how to become a pilot.*
- What do I want to learn about this topic?
    - *I want to learn how old you must be to become a pilot.*
    - *I want to learn how pilots know how to fly.*

During Reading:

- I wonder why...
    - *I wonder why pilots wear hats.*
    - *I wonder if flying a helicopter is more difficult than flying a plane.*
- What have I learned so far?
    - *I have learned that there are big and small planes.*
    - *I have learned that a pilot uses a map.*

After Reading:

- What details did I learn about this topic?
    - *I have learned that some pilots fly helicopters.*
    - *I have learned that pilots wear uniforms.*
- Read the book again and look for the vocabulary words.
    - *I see the word **helicopter** on page 9 and the word **uniforms** on page 12. The other vocabulary words are found on page 14.*

This is a **pilot**.

Many pilots fly big **planes**.

Some pilots fly
little planes.

XTRA 260

This pilot can fly a **helicopter**.

This pilot uses a **map** to help fly through the sky.

All pilots wear **uniforms**!

Word List

Sight Words

a	is	this
all	little	through
big	many	to
can	sky	uses
fly	some	
help	the	

Words to Know

helicopter

map

pilot

planes

uniforms

35 Words

This is a **pilot**.

Many pilots fly big **planes**.

Some pilots fly little planes.

This pilot can fly a **helicopter**.

This pilot uses a **map** to help fly through the sky.

All pilots wear **uniforms**!

People I Meet PILOT

Written by: Douglas Bender
Designed by: Rhea Wallace
Series Development: James Earley
Proofreader: Janine Deschenes
Educational Consultant: Marie Lemke M.Ed.

Photographs:
Shutterstock: Svitlana Hulko: cover, p. 1; Natalia Bostan: p. 3; joo830908: p. 4-5; Vladislav Sinelnikov: p. 7; pio3: p. 8; schame: p. 11; Lightfield Studios: p. 13

Crabtree Publishing

crabtreebooks.com 800-387-7650

Printed in the U.S.A./012023/
CG20220815

Published in Canada
Crabtree Publishing
616 Welland Ave.
St. Catharines, Ontario
L2M 5V6

Published in the United States
Crabtree Publishing
347 Fifth Ave
Suite 1402-145
New York, NY 10016

Library and Archives Canada Cataloguing in Publication
Available at Library and Archives Canada

Library of Congress Cataloging-in-Publication Data
Available at the Library of Congress

Hardcover: 978-1-0396-9638-9
Paperback: 978-1-0396-9745-4
Ebook (pdf): 978-1-0396-9959-5
Epub: 978-1-0396-9852-9